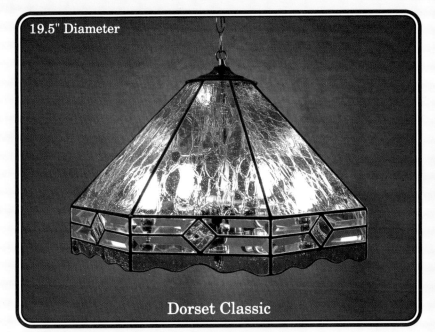

19.5" Diameter

Dorset Classic

CW00407663

N ... S

25 FULL ... DES

10" Wide

South Park Sconce

15" Diameter

Victoria Cone

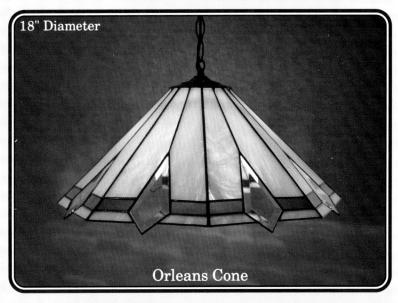

18" Diameter

Orleans Cone

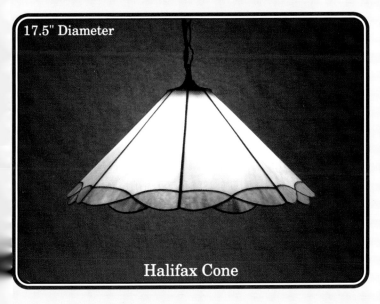

17.5" Diameter

Halifax Cone

17 "Diameter

Falaise Cone

Wardell

PUBLICATIONS

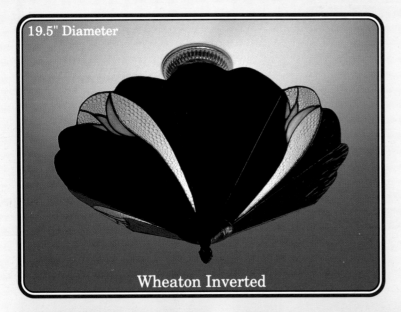

19.5" Diameter

Wheaton Inverted

13.5 "Diameter

Wollaston Northern Lights

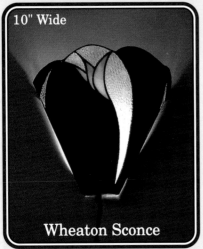

10" Wide

Wheaton Sconce

7.5" Diameter

Sherbrooke Cone

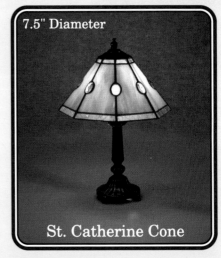

7.5" Diameter

St. Catherine Cone

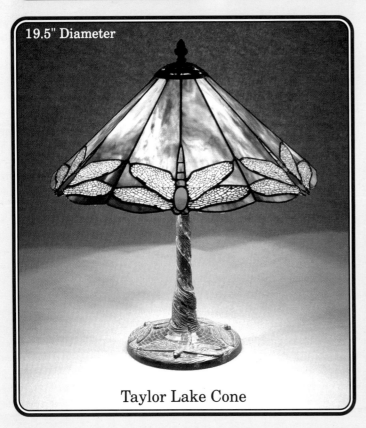

19.5" Diameter

Taylor Lake Cone

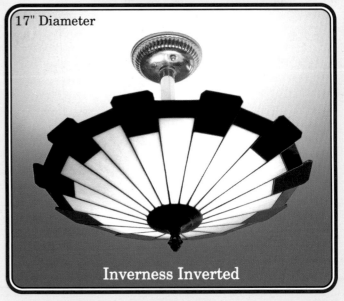

17" Diameter

Inverness Inverted

21" Diameter

Regent Pavilion

11.5" Diameter

Hampton Cone

9" Diameter

Navaho Cone

18" Diameter

Parkdale Inverted

13.5 " Diameter

Doran Classic

8" Diameter

Willow Mini-classic

13.5" Diameter

South Park Square

Wardell
PUBLICATIONS INC

Instruction, Inspiration and Innovation for the Art Glass Communnity

    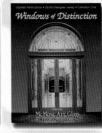 

e-mail: info@wardellpublications.com   website: www.wardellpublications.com

NORTHERN SHADES

25 FULL-SIZE PATTERNS FOR STAINED GLASS LAMPSHADES

Lampshade Designers

Brian Eagle
Donna Edmondson
Stephan Gray
Gisele Johnson
Barbara Pickthorne
Ed Kerzner

Graphics and Layout

Randy Wardell

Photography

Randy Wardell
Judy Huffman

Editor & Publisher

Randy Wardell

Special Thanks

Steve Hanes
Annabelle Wenzel
Kathleen Eagle
Monika Van der Veer
Dan Parker Chapman

Printed in Canada

Published by

Wardell
PUBLICATIONS INC

To receive our electronic newsletter or to send suggestions please contact us
by EMail at: info@wardellpublications.com or visit or web site at: www.wardellpublications.com

A Letter from the Designers

Welcome to the Northern Art Glass lamp pattern book. We are a full service, stained glass studio, located in the heart of Canada's national capital - Ottawa, Ontario. Our production includes stained glass design and fabrication as well as sandblasting, painting, kiln-work, acid etching and whatever the customer requires. As designers and craftspeople we have a reputation for innovative glasswork in both traditional and contemporary motifs for all manner of windows, doors, interior screens and of course, our popular lampshades.

Our teaching staff offers instruction courses for all levels of crafters in stained glass. We have drawn on this experience to bring to this book tried and proven lamp patterns, complete with our most popular color combinations for each design.

Stained glass, with its unique and wondrous qualities, has unlimited potential to enhance any environment. The perfect pattern, combined with the careful selection of glass, can provide either a subtle ambience or become a stunning focal point depending on your requirements.

The next time you find yourself drawn to the challenge of a new product, with mounting excitement and an uncontrollable urge to cut some glass, we think you will find some inspiration in the 25 lamp designs contained in Northern Shades.

Happy cutting!

All the Gang at Northern Art Glass

Please visit our website at: www.northernartglass.com

Cataloguing in Publication Data
Main entry under title:

Northern Shades: Full-siz Patterns for Stained Glass Lampshades
Eagle, Brian 1953-
ISBN-13: 978-0-919985-43-8
ISBN-10: 0-919985-43-2

1. Lampshades, Glass-Patterns
2. Glass painting and staining - Patterns
3. Glass craft - Patterns
NK5440.L3E34 1991 749'.63 C91-094314-1

Notice: Due to differing conditions, materials and skill levels, the publisher, author and material manufacturers disclaim any liability for unsatisfactory results or injury due to improper use of tools, materials or information contained in this publication.
Trade named tools and products, manufactured materials and/or proprietary processes mentioned or photographed for this publication are Trademarked™ and Copyrighted© by the respective manufacturers. All rights reserved.

Printed in Canada by Printcrafters Ltd.
Published simultaneously in Canada and USA
E-mail: info@wardellpublications.com
Website: www.wardellpublications.com

Northern Shades is Copyright© 2006 by Wardell Publications Inc

Northern Shades was first Published & Copyright© 1991 by Wardell Publications

Northern Shades is exclusively published by Wardell Publications, Inc. ALL RIGHTS RESERVED. No part of this publication may be reproduced or used for any reason or by any means, whether graphic, electronic, or mechanical, including photocopying, digital scanning, recording, taping, or information storage & retrieval systems or otherwise, without the prior permission in writing from the publisher.

The text, layout and designs of this book, as well as the book in its entirety, are protected by the copyright laws of the United States (17 U.S.C. 101 et seq.) and similar laws in other countries.

Wardell Publications Inc. in partnership with Northern Art Glass and the Pattern Designers (as named on each pattern info page), grants limited permission to produce a work(s) from the designs contained in this book, for personal use only (not for commercial resale), provided that the production quantity does not exceed more than five (5) units derived from any design contained herein. This permission does not extend to the reproduction or reprinting, whether re-drawn, enlarged or otherwise altered, for distribution or any other use, of any pattern, drawing, photograph, or text contained in this book, or of the book as a whole.

Commercial production of works based in part or in whole upon the designs contained in this book is strictly forbidden without the prior written permission of the publisher. Please consult the copyright section of our website http://www.wardellpublications.com for information on how to obtain permission to produce a work(s) from any book, pattern or design published by Wardell Publications Inc. and offer it for commercial resale.

CONTENTS

PAGE

FULL-SIZE LAMPSHADE PATTERNS

FULL-SIZE LAMPSHADE PATTERNS

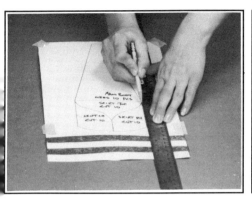

Step 1: Trace the pattern, making two copies, one on standard paper and one on card stock paper.

First — Cut completely around the perimeter (outside) lines of the lamp pattern, following the center of each line.

Second — Cut the interior design line following the center of each line. This will align each section to match the pattern above and below it.

Step 2: Carefully trace the pattern onto the glass using a felt-tip pen and cut the glass piece by scoring on the inside of the marker line. *You must always cut the line away* so the marker line is on the waste glass when you break it off. Check your glass piece with the pattern to verify that they are exactly the same size and shape. If the glass is not exact, you must grind it or cut it. Adjust your scoring to be more precise when scoring the next piece. Continue cutting your glass until all pieces are complete.

NOTE: When a pattern calls for Cut 1 Up 1 Down, you are required to trace and cut the glass with pattern facing you, **OVERTURN** pattern and trace and cut the glass with pattern facing down.

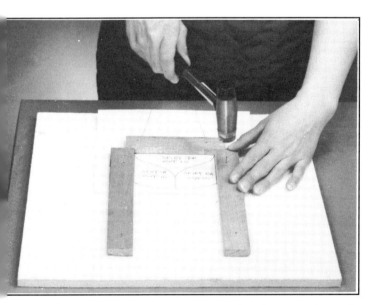

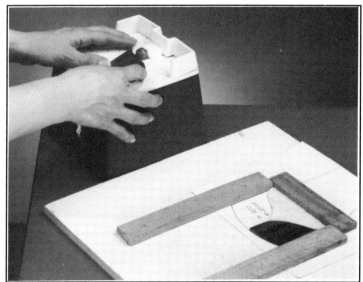

Step 3: When constructing a lamp that has panels with interior designs (a flat section containing two or more pieces), they must be fitted and assembled in a jig. Lay the working drawing (paper copy) of the pattern on your work table, face up. Nail three pieces of glazing lath onto your drawing so the outside line of the section to be assembled is half showing.

Step 4: Place one set of glass pieces into the jig as your drawing shows. If the pieces do not fit accurately, you will have to groze or grind them to fit or cut new ones. When the pieces fit into the jig correctly, clean each piece of glass and copper foil it.

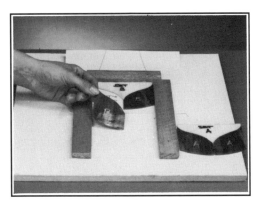

NOTE: If you intend to grind and fit all panel sets before foiling and assembling, you must code each set before removing them from the jig and keep the matched sets together.

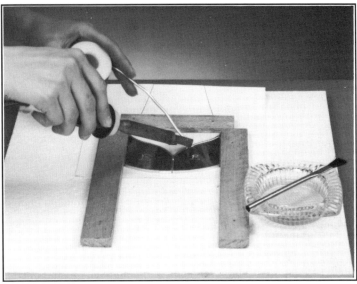

Step 5: Place the foiled glass pieces back into the jig and flat solder them. Remove the panel from the jig, turn it over and flat solder the other side. Finish by running a solder bead on the face side. Repeat for all panels.

Step 6: Start the lamp assembly with the row that is called the main body. This is the large section closest to the vase cap opening. Lay these pieces face side up on the work bench in a semi-circle. Use black plastic electrical tape (or in a pinch, masking tape) and tape the sections together. The areas where tape will come in contact with the glass *must be* clean or the tape will not adhere.

Step 7: Carefully raise this row up into a cone shape, keeping the large diameter end on the bench. Bring the two adjoining side sections together and tape.

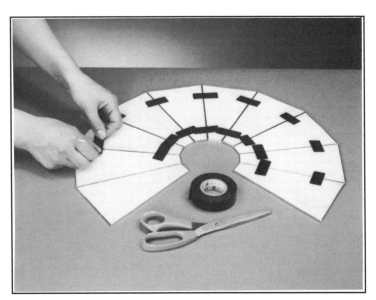

EXCEPTION: When constructing a lamp which has several rows that make up the main body (eg. dome style lamp), the top row is often at a very flat angle which makes it difficult to raise into a cone shape. In a case such as this choose a row with a greater angle (perhaps the second row) as the start row and proceed as above. Be sure to add the top row and vase cap next for greater strength.

Step 8: You must be sure the bottom of the cone is *flat* on the bench. Flux and tack solder each seam at the bottom corner by applying a small dab of molten solder with the tip of your iron.

Step 9: Flux and solder completely around the top opening. Flat solder down the outside of each seam as best you can (leaving tape on) to strengthen the assembly.

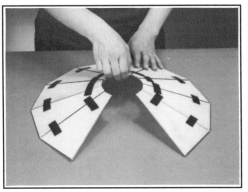
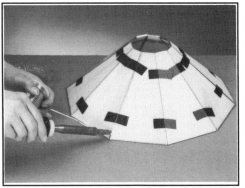
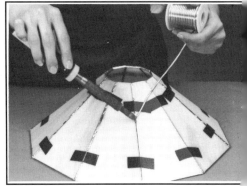

8

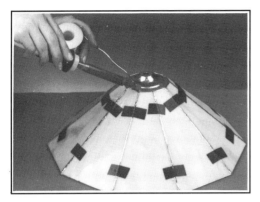

Step 10 : You have probably noticed how flimsy the lamp is at this stage. Attach the vase cap or spider now to strengthen its form (see Page 12 &13). The bottom must be sitting flat on the table when installing the vase cap to ensure the lamp has a proper shape. When the cap is soldered securely to the outside, carefully turn the lamp over and solder all inside seams and around the vase cap.

Step 11: Place your lamp upside down into a soldering box. (A cardboard box with newspapers loosely crumpled inside.) The assembly will continue by adding the panels of the next row (in the example shown it is the skirt or bottom row). Position and tack solder the first panel of this row to the main body.

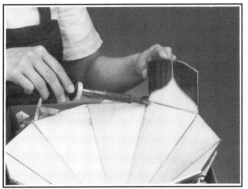

Step 12: Place the second panel beside the first and tack it to the main body. Position pieces one and two until the seam meets evenly and tack solder together.

Step 13: Continue by adding the remaining panels in order around the lamp, tacking one to the other as you go. When the complete row is assembled, flat solder all the inside seams before moving on. Continue to add rows (if necessary) until the lower lamp is complete. Finish by soldering completely around the bottom edge for more strength and stability.

Step 14: Turn the lamp right side up in the soldering box. If you are constructing a lamp with a crown (upper most row) use the same procedure as described for the skirt assembly in Step 11, 12 & 13.

Step 15: The lamp should be completely assembled now and ready for final soldering. Remove all remaining tape. Position the lamp in the soldering box and level the seam you intend to solder (horizontal to the floor). Take your time and run a bead of solder. If the molten solder is flowing away from the seam or appears to be running downhill, this indicates the seam is not perfectly level. Reposition the lamp in the box and resume soldering.

HINT: If you are trying to fill a gap (a space between two foiled pieces), and the molten solder falls through, cover the space from the inside with masking tape to keep the solder from dripping.

Step 16: When you have completed soldering, do a quality check of all seams inside and out to make sure they are finished and uniform. Fine bead soldering is a difficult skill to master, don't be discouraged, remember practice makes perfect.

To finish your lamp, solder a wire around the bottom edge. For instruction and details see Page 14.
To clean your project of flux and solder residue use a glass cleaner, see Page 14.
To apply antique patina to the solder beads (a coppery or black color), see Page 14.

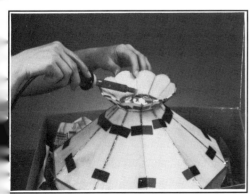

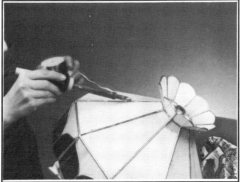

ALTERNATE LAMP ASSEMBLY METHOD

Instead of the row assembly described earlier, an alternative used by many crafters is a system called row-on-row assembly. To use this method, substitute steps 11, 12, 13 & 14 in lamp assembly description.

Step 11: Place your lamp upside down into a soldering box. (A cardboard box with newspapers loosely crumpled inside as shown.) The assembly will continue by adding the panels of the next row (in the example shown it is the skirt or bottom row). Lay these panels in sequence, side by side and face up on your bench.

EXCEPTION: As the angle of the sections increase, as happens in very small lamps or lamps with only 6 or 8 sides, the tape can become very tight and may not stretch sufficiently. Try putting the tape on the back-side instead of the face-side.

Tape them together in the same manner as you taped the main body. Gently lift the row on its edge, bend it around into a circle and tape the ends together. Tack solder all seams at top and bottom corners only.

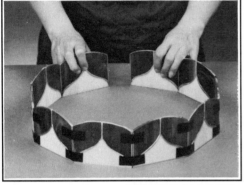

Step 12: Your main body section should be upside down in the soldering box. Gently lift the skirt and place it on the main body. The seam corners of the two sections must line up one to the other. Tack solder the sections together at these corners.

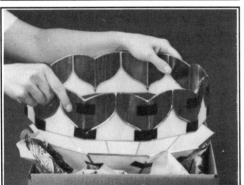

Step 13: When the complete row is attached, flat solder all the inside seams for more strength and stability before moving on.

Step 14: Turn the lamp right side up in the soldering box. If you are constructing a lamp with a crown (upper most row) use the same procedure as for the skirt assembly in Steps 11, 12 & 13.

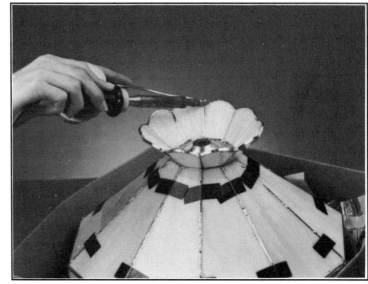

JOINER PIECES

Some lampshades must have glass (joiner) pieces inserted to join the sections once the shade has been assembled. A joiner piece usually bridges a gap between two sections which are attached at an angle to one another.

Step 1. Place the pattern for the joiner piece in the appropriate space to see if the size is satisfactory. If the pattern correctly fits the space, cut out the glass piece. In most cases the pattern will not fit well. This is due to inevitable variations in glass cutting and assembly angle.

Step 2. If the pattern fit is unacceptable you must make a new pattern of the space by placing a piece of pattern card underneath the hole and tracing around it with a marking pen. Cut the glass for the joiner piece according to this new pattern.
NOTE: Verify the size of each space individually with the pattern before cutting the glass.

 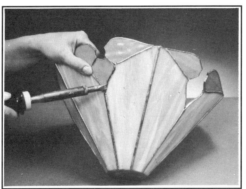 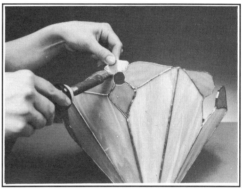

Step 3. Fit the glass piece into its designated space by grinding or grozing as necessary. Wrap the piece with copper foil. Insert it into the space so the edges are flush with the adjacent sections and tack solder it. Do not be too concerned if all edges are not completely flush since that is virtually impossible.

Step 4. Verify the pattern for the next joiner piece and cut the glass piece. Wrap it with copper foil, insert into place and tack solder it. Repeat this procedure for each joiner piece until all are installed. Finish the seams with a solder bead.

INVERTED LAMP INSTALLATION

WARNING: When wiring and installing your lamp you must consider all federal and local electrical codes and regulations.
The most common method of installing an inverted shade is by using a standard 2 or 3 way bulb fixture. Often you will find this type of fixture already installed in your home. It consists of a canopy, the bulb fixture, a threaded nipple extender and a lock nut & finial (see drawing). The fixture is hard wired (permanently) to the ceiling electrical box (see warning above) and the inverted stained glass lampshade is attached to the nipple, between the locknut and the finial. You must adjust the length of the nipple according to the depth of the shade (a deeper shade will require a longer nipple). When choosing a bulb fixture, be sure to obtain one with riveted brackets. This will ensure proper strength to support heavy glass shades.

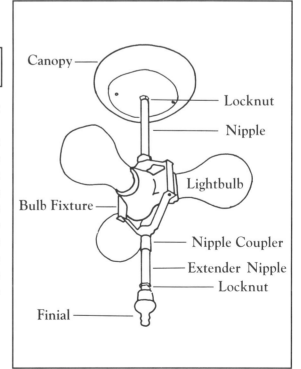

Canopy —

Locknut

Nipple

Lightbulb

Bulb Fixture —

Nipple Coupler

Extender Nipple

Locknut

Finial —

11

HANGING HARDWARE

1. Lamp Hanging Hardware:
This is an integral part of a lampshade. It must be securely soldered to the top opening of a lampshade to solidify the structure and to provide hanging support for the electrical hardware. There are many different types of hanging hardware available, we will describe the two most common:

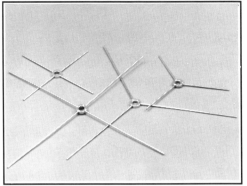

SPIDER

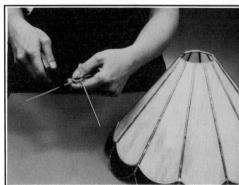

This is a brass ring about one inch in diameter with 3 or 4 arms radiating out from 6" to 12". The number of arms must divide evenly into the number of sides of your shade. For example, a six-sided shade requires a 3 arm spider while an eight-sided shade requires a 4 arm spider.

Installation:

Step 1: To ensure the spider hole is centered, measure the top opening of your lampshade and divide this dimension by two. For example, a 4" opening divided by two is 2". Measure this distance from the center of the spider's central-hole down an arm and mark with a pen. Measure and mark all arms.

Step 2: Use a pair of pliers to bend the arms down at the marks. The angle of the bend must match the top angle of the lampshade. The first trial bend is simply a guess at the correct angle.

Step 3: Gently turn the lamp upside down and test the arm angles by positioning and centering the spider in the shade opening. Adjust the angles as needed. Each arm should extend approximately two to four inches from the top of the opening and straight down each seam, cut them shorter if necessary.

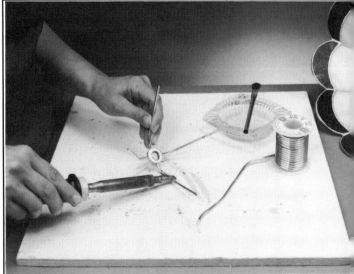

Step 4: When the spider fits the opening correctly, remove and tin each arm from the bend to the outside tip. Position and center the spider into the shade opening and solder the arms securely down the inside seams.

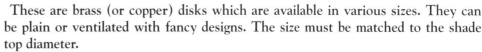

VASE CAPS

These are brass (or copper) disks which are available in various sizes. They can be plain or ventilated with fancy designs. The size must be matched to the shade top diameter.

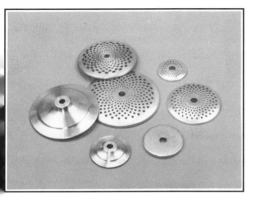

INSTALLATION

Step 1: To install a cap properly it should fit just inside the shade opening. This will ensure that it is soldered securely to the vertical seams of the lampshade. Vase caps are manufactured in standard sizes and often the shade opening is an odd size. Most vase caps can be cut down with sheet metal shears to custom fit the opening.

Step 2: If you were unable to find a cap to fit the shade opening exactly, choose a cap which is slightly larger than the opening. To mark the cap for trimming, place it on the shade opening from the outside and use a felt-tip pen to trace around the opening from the inside.

Step 3: Trim the cap following the traced line with sheet metal shears (tin snips). Place the cap back on the shade to check the fit and adjust as necessary.

Step 4: The outside surface of the vase cap should be *tinned* with a thin layer of solder before installation. Tinning will allow antique patina (see Page 14) to color the cap the same as the rest of the solder seams. It will also make soldering the cap to the shade easier.

NOTE: Since the vase cap draws heat away from the soldering area (referred to as heatsinking) it is more difficult to make the solder flow. To ensure a smooth finish, more time will be required to heat both solder and metal while tinning.

Step 5: Position the cap on the shade opening and tack solder it. The cap must be centered and level on the shade. When the fit is correct, solder around the cap inside and out.

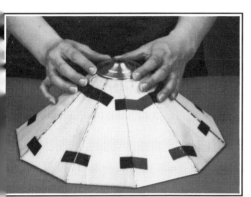

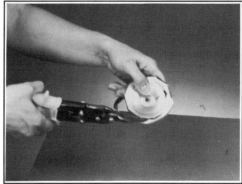

NOTE: If you are constructing a large shade, you can combine a cap and a spider for added strength.

WARNING: When wiring and installing your lamp you must consider all federal and local electrical codes and regulations.

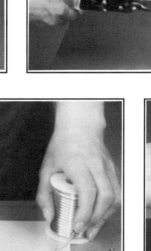

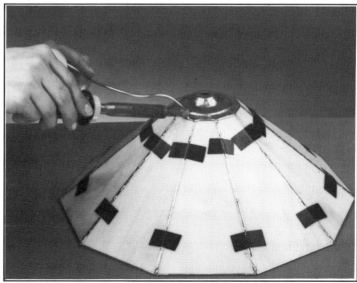

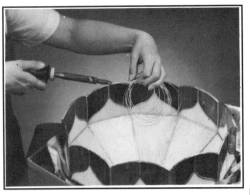

WIRE SUPPORT AROUND BOTTOM OF LAMP

It is recommended that a wire (14-18 gauge, brass or copper) be soldered around the bottom edge of your lamp for reinforcement. This wire will help to finish the bottom edge and holds it firmly together. Tack solder one piece of wire completely around the bottom edge and overlap the ends at least 1/2 inch. Finish the edge with a solder bead.

ANTIQUE PATINA

Best results are achieved when patina is applied to solder immediately after it is completed and cleaned with glass cleaner. Rub the solder using a soft rag or brush soaked with the liquid patina. Clean the solution from the glass immediately. Wear rubber gloves while handling this solution. If your project has been finished for a few days, you must scrub down all the soldered seams with fine steel wool or a metal pot scrubber and clean to remove all corrosion before applying the patina.

CLEANING YOUR PROJECT

It is very important to clean your project as soon as you have finished working on it. If the flux is left on, it will corrode the solder even overnight. This will make touch-up soldering or final clean-up difficult. Any good quality glass cleaner will work, as will a solution of vinegar and water.

If the solder has corroded and is difficult to solder they can be cleaned by scrubbing with fine steel wool or a small wire brush. Caution: If you have already applied antique patina to the solder, scrubbing will remove it.

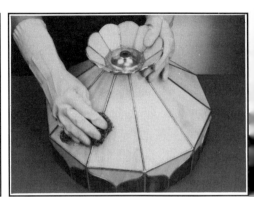

POLISHING OR WAXING

To preserve the shiny finish on the solder after a patina has been applied, use a good quality spray furniture polish. Apply the polish and rub all solder seams vigorously. For an even shinier finish, polish the patina with a jeweler's rouge cloth or use a brass or silver polish. Finish with an application of car wax. You can even polish the wax with a power car polisher.

PHOTOCOPYING YOUR PATTERNS

In recent years the photocopier has come into very wide use for many applications. Local copy centers are opening everywhere, offering services that include enlarging and reducing your originals. This opens up a multitude of possibilities for the stained glass crafter to alter the size of patterns quickly and easily. Enlarging is especially useful for free-form projects such as sun catchers or small panels due to the limitation in size, depending on the photocopier used.

There is, however, one note of caution concerning the use of photocopiers (other than possible copyright infringement). Most photocopiers do not make exact copies of the original. While the copy is very close, the mechanics of the copying process introduces some amount of distortion that can be disastrous when constructing a three-dimensional project such as a lampshade. The distortion usually results in a slight enlargement (or reduction) of the pattern in the vertical dimension to a greater degree than in the horizontal dimension. This does not mean you cannot use a photocopier for your lamp patterns, but it does mean you must carefully measure each pattern component to verify that they will fit one to the other.

WINDSOR   by Barbara Pickthorne

PROJECT 1

DEGREE OF DIFFICULTY

1	2	**3**	4	5

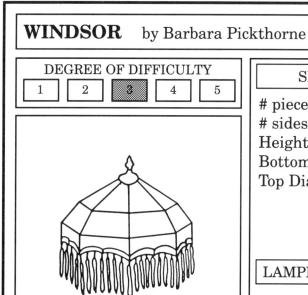

SPECIFICATIONS

# pieces—	40
# sides—	8
Height (incl. prisms)—	8" (24 cm)
Bottom Dia.—	10" (25cm)
Top Dia.—	2" (5 cm)

LAMPBASE INFORMATION

Base height—	9"
Harp size—	6"

MATERIALS

— 1 1/2 sq. ft. Solid Dark Green
— 3 /4 sq. ft. Textured Clear
PRISMS — 48 - 3" long Cast Glass Prisms
— 2" Vase Cap

PROJECT INFORMATION: Fully finish your lamp, patina and clean before attaching the bottom row of prisms. These are inexpensive cast glass prisms (not crystal) which are available from your stained glass supply shop or from a household lighting fixture store. Usually they have an octagon prism attached to a tear drop prism by a wire loop (see diagram on page 16). These prisms can be used as purchased or modified by removing the octagon prism and attaching a short length (7/8") of jewel box chain to the existing wire loop (as shown in the color photograph). It is important to solder the prisms to the skirt at the horizontal trim band seam 1/2" from the bottom edge (never attach them to the bottom foil edge). See diagram on page 16 for prism placement.

HAMPTON   by Brian Eagle

PROJECT 2

DEGREE OF DIFFICULTY

1	**2**	3	4	5

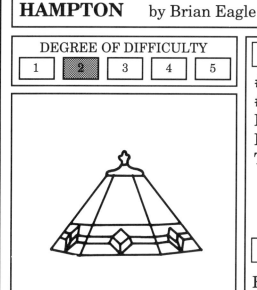

SPECIFICATIONS

# pieces—	60
# sides—	6
Height—	7" (18cm)
Bottom Dia.-	11 1/2" (30 cm)
Top Dia.—	3 1/2" (9 cm)

LAMPBASE INFORMATION

Base height—	8 3/4"
Harp size—	7 1/2"

MATERIALS

— 2 sq. ft. White Opal
— 1 sq. ft. Irid. Blue Opal
— 1/3 sq. ft. Textured Clear Sparkle
— Bevels 6 - 1" x 1"
—3 1/2 " Vase Cap

PROJECT INFORMATION: Always place the bevels that you have purchased on your pattern and adjust the surrounding pieces where necessary to ensure an accurate fit. After copper foiling we recommend covering both sides of the bevels with masking tape (leaving the foil exposed) to protect them from scratches during assembly.

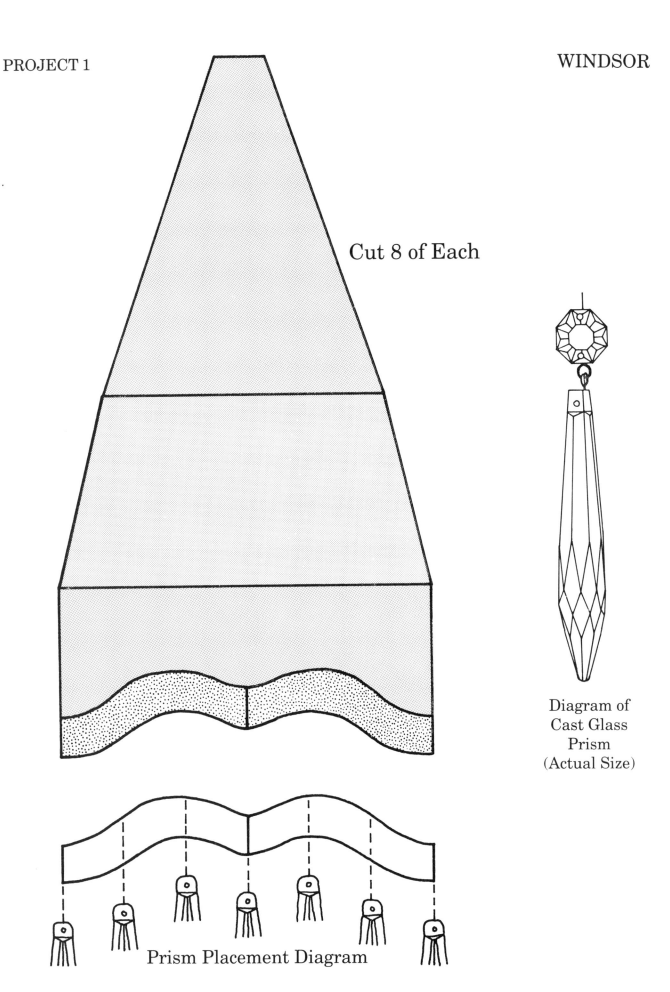

Cut 8 of Each

Diagram of
Cast Glass
Prism
(Actual Size)

Prism Placement Diagram

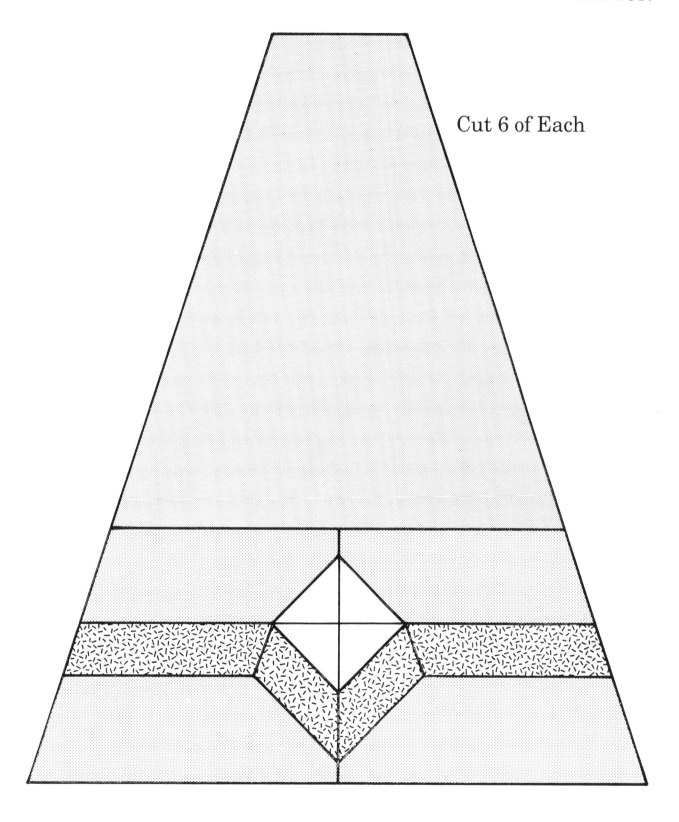

Cut 6 of Each

STE. CATHERINE by Gisele Johnson

DEGREE OF DIFFICULTY

1	2	3	4	5

SPECIFICATIONS

# pieces—	32
# sides—	8
Height—	5" (13 cm)
Bottom Dia.—	7 3/4" (20cm)
Top Dia.—	2 1/2" (6 cm)

LAMPBASE

Base height—	5 1/2"
Harp size—	4"

MATERIALS

 — 1/2 sq. ft. Textured Clear

 — 3/4 sq. ft. Iridescent Blue Opal

JEWELS — 8 - 18mm x 25mm Clear Oval Jewels

 — 2 1/2 " Vase Cap

PROJECT INFORMATION: If a jewel does not fit easily into its space, you can grind its edge, but be careful not to chip it . For more information on Joiner Pieces see page 11. The top opening can be fitted with a 2 1/2" vase cap as shown on page 13.

SHERBROOKE by Gisele Johnson

DEGREE OF DIFFICULTY

1	2	3	4	5

SPECIFICATIONS

# pieces—	32
# sides—	8
Height—	5" (13 cm)
Bottom Dia.—	7 3/4" (20cm)
Top Dia.—	2 1/2" (6 cm)

LAMPBASE

Base height—	5 1/2"
Harp size—	4"

MATERIALS

 — 3/4 sq. ft. Blue/Mauve Opal

— 1/2 sq. ft. Textured Mauve Cath.

 — 2 1/2 " Vase Cap

PROJECT INFORMATION: The top opening can be fitted with a 2 1/2" vase cap as shown on page 13.

NAVAHO by Stephan Gray

DEGREE OF DIFFICULTY

1	2	3	4	5

SPECIFICATIONS

# pieces—	72
# sides—	6
Height—	7" (18 cm)
Bottom Dia.—	9" (23 cm)
Top Dia.—	2 1/2" (6 cm)

LAMPBASE

Base height—	5"
Harp size—	6"

MATERIALS

— 1 1/2 sq. ft. Iridescent Black

— 3/4 sq. ft. Turquoise

— 1 sq. ft. Lt. Cranberry Cathedral

— Small Piece Dk. Cranberry Cathedral

— 2 1/2 " Vase Cap

PROJECT INFORMATION: The top opening can be fitted with a 2 1/2" vase cap as shown on page 13.

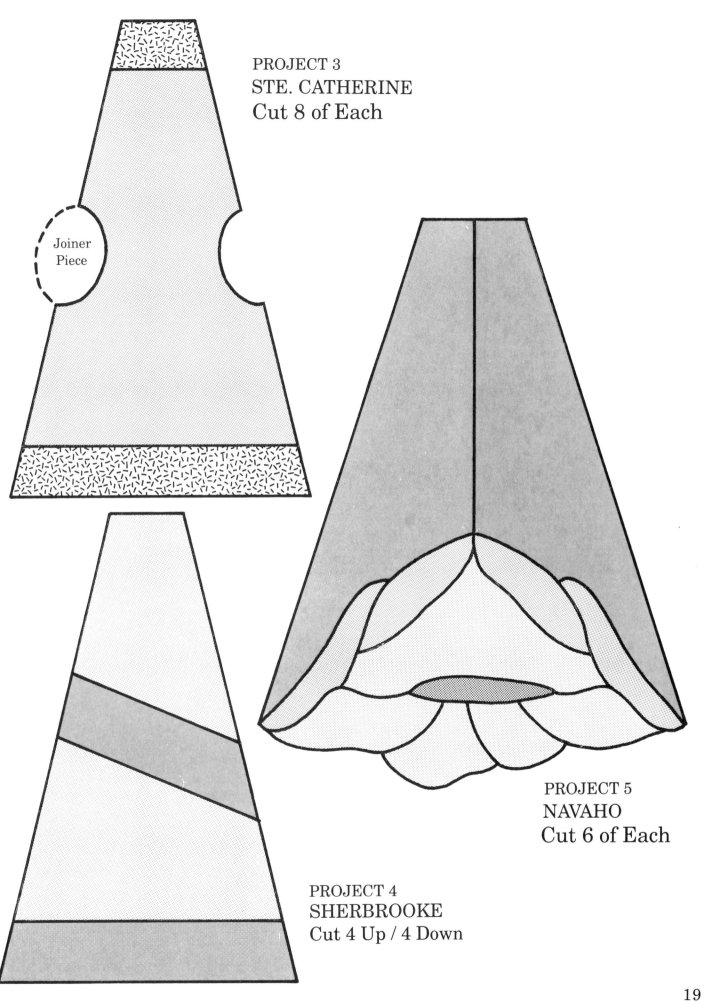

PROJECT 3
STE. CATHERINE
Cut 8 of Each

Joiner
Piece

PROJECT 5
NAVAHO
Cut 6 of Each

PROJECT 4
SHERBROOKE
Cut 4 Up / 4 Down

19

PARKDALE   by Brian Eagle

PROJECT 6

DEGREE OF DIFFICULTY

1	2	3	4	5

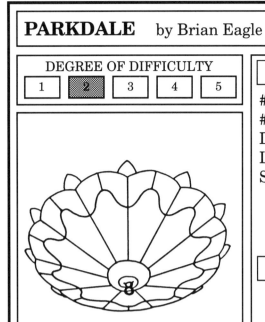

SPECIFICATIONS

# pieces—	44
# sides—	11
Depth—	5" (13 cm)
Large Dia.—	18" (46 cm)
Small Dia.—	3 1/2" (9 cm)

PATTERN INFORMATION

Pattern on page 21

MATERIALS

— 1 1/2 sq. ft.
Dark Blue Opal

— 1 1/2 sq. ft.
White/Amber/Blue Opal

— 3 1/2 " Vase Cap

PROJECT INFORMATION: We recommend that a reinforcement wire be soldered along the outside edge to give the lamp extra strength (see page 14). A brass ball chain (the type used on electrical pull-chain sockets) can be substituted for the wire for a more decorative effect. For Inverted Lamp Installation see page 11.

SUSSEX   by Brian Eagle

PROJECT 7

DEGREE OF DIFFICULTY

1	2	3	4	5

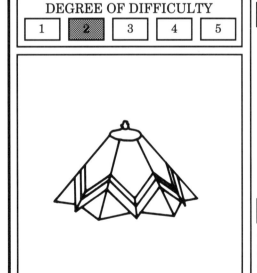

SPECIFICATIONS

# pieces—	42
# sides—	6
Height—	6 1/2" (17 cm)
Bottom Dia.—	12" (31 cm)
Top Dia.—	3 1/2" (9 cm)

LAMPBASE INFORMATION

Base height—	8 3/4"
Harp size—	7"

MATERIALS

— 1 1/2 sq. ft.
Pastel Green Opal

— 1/2 sq. ft.
White Opal

— 1/2 sq. ft.
Pink Opal

— Bevels
12 - 3"x3"x3" Triangles

— 3 1/2 " Vase Cap

PROJECT INFORMATION: Always place the bevels that you have purchased on your pattern and adjust the surrounding pieces where necessary to ensure an accurate fit. After copper foiling we recommend covering both sides of the bevels with masking tape (leaving the foil exposed) to protect them from scratches during assembly.

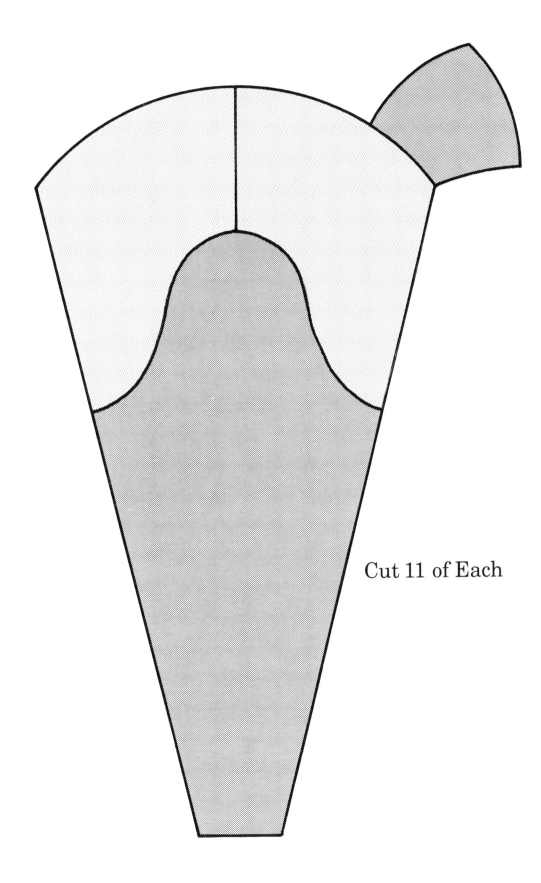

Cut 11 of Each

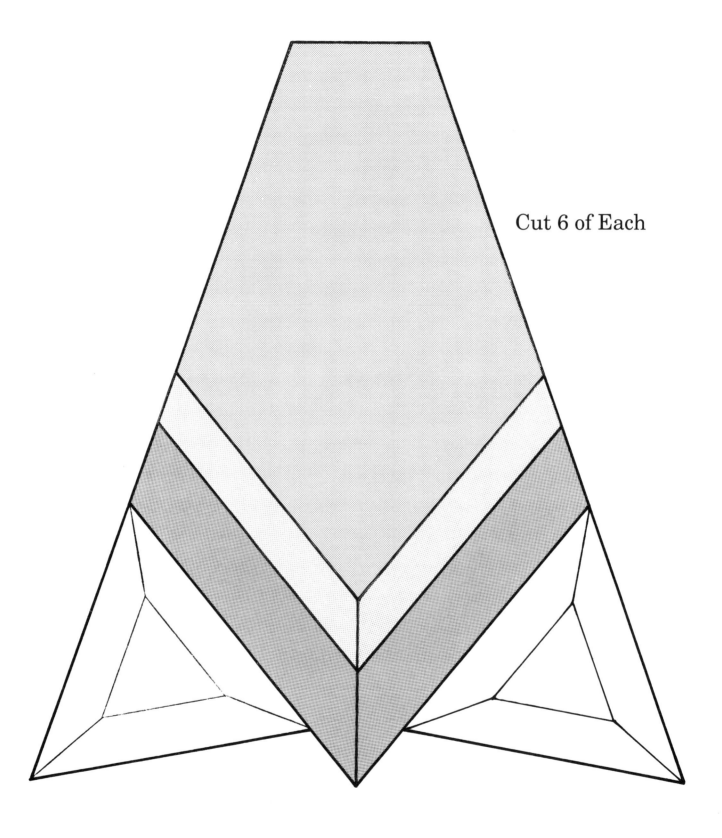

Cut 6 of Each

WILLOW — by Donna Edmondson

DEGREE OF DIFFICULTY

1	2	3	4	5

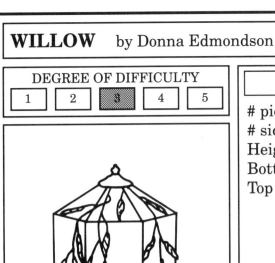

SPECIFICATIONS

# pieces—	42
# sides—	7
Height—	8 1/2" (22 cm)
Bottom Dia.—	8" (20 cm)
Top Dia.—	2 1/2" (6 cm)

LAMPBASE INFORMATION

Base height—	8"
Harp size—	7"

MATERIALS

 — 3 1/4 sq. ft. Dark Green Opal

 — 1/2 sq. ft. Light Green Opal

- - - - 4 ft. - 14 gauge copper wire

 — 2 1/2 " Vase Cap

PROJECT INFORMATION: The level 3 degree of difficulty is due to the delicate point on the main body panel. Tin the edges of the leaf overlays and spot solder them to a tinned copper wire as shown on the pattern page. Clean the lamp and overlays and spot solder to the seams of the lampshade as shown in the color photograph or create your own placement. Carefully lift each leaf slightly and place a drop of clear silicone or white glue underneath.

INVERNESS — by Brian Eagle

DEGREE OF DIFFICULTY

1	2	3	4	5

SPECIFICATIONS

# pieces—	40
# sides—	20
Depth—	4 1/2" (11 cm)
Large Dia.—	17" (43 cm)
Small Dia.—	3 1/2" (9 cm)

PATTERN INFORMATION

Pattern on Page 25

MATERIALS

 — 2 sq. ft. Iridescent White Opal

— 1 1/2 sq. ft. Black Opal

 — 3 1/2 " Vase Cap

PROJECT INFORMATION: Solder each individual panel and tape the horizontal seam on both sides for more stability in final assembly. For more information on Lamp Assembly see pages 8 - 10. It is recommended that a reinforcement wire be soldered along the outside edge to give the lamp extra strength (see page 14). A brass ball chain (the type used on electrical pull-chain sockets) can be substituted for the wire for a more decorative effect. For Inverted Lamp Installation see page 11.

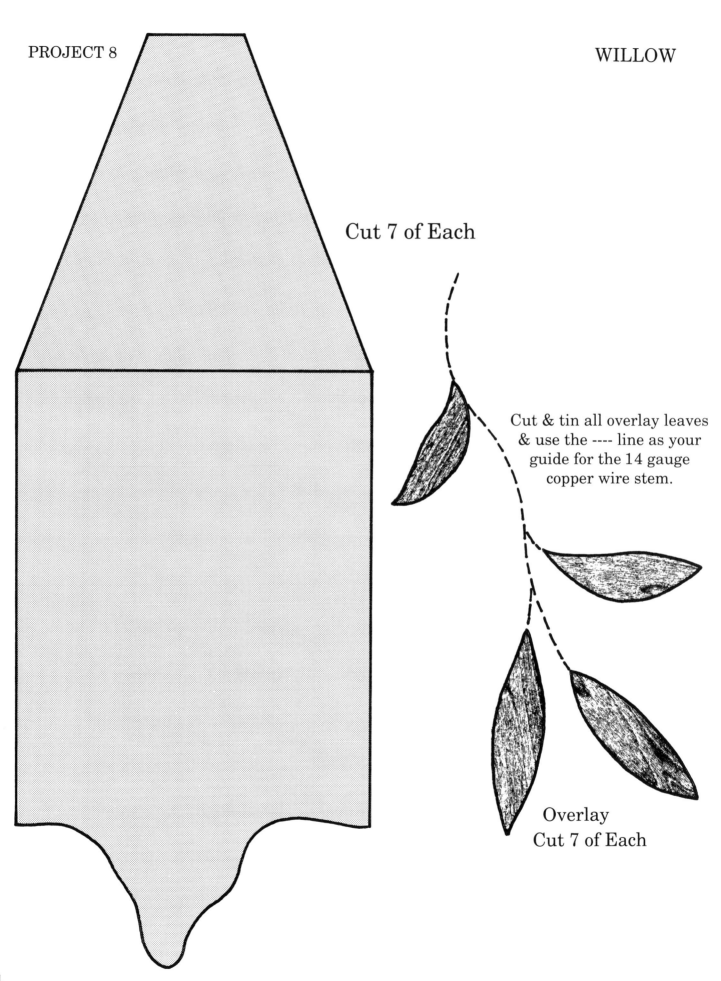

Cut 7 of Each

Cut & tin all overlay leaves
& use the ---- line as your
guide for the 14 gauge
copper wire stem.

Overlay
Cut 7 of Each

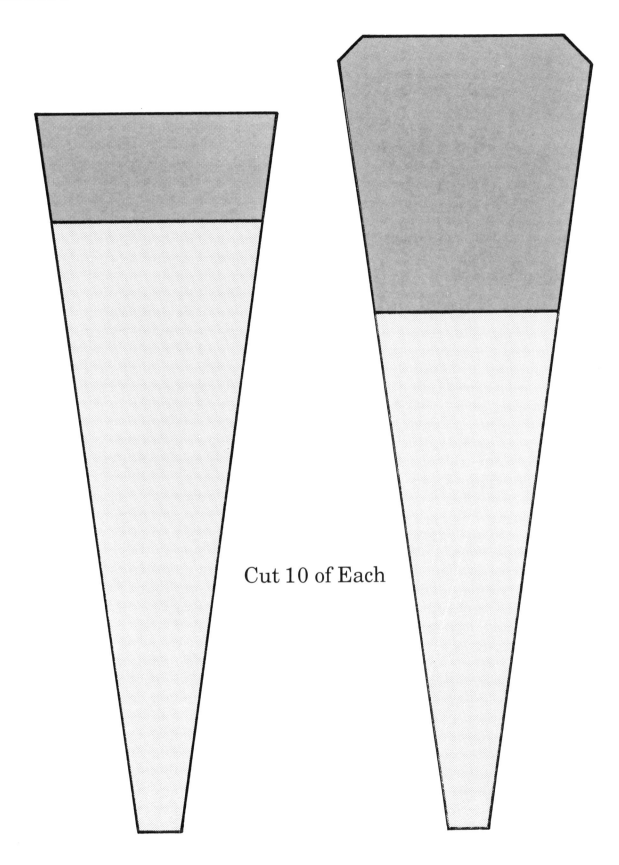

Cut 10 of Each

TAYLOR LAKE   by Donna Edmondson

DEGREE OF DIFFICULTY

1	2	3	**4**	5

SPECIFICATIONS

# pieces—	102
# sides—	12
Height—	8 1/2" (22 cm)
Bottom Dia.—	19 1/2"(50cm)
Top Dia.—	4" (10 cm)

LAMPBASE

Base height—	12 1/2"
Harp size—	9"

MATERIALS

- — 6 sq. ft. Purple/Blue/White Opal
- — 2 sq. ft. White Opal
- — 1/3 sq. ft. Streaky Green/Brown
- —Small Piece Green Cathedral
- FILIGREE —6 Pair Dragonfly Wing Filigree

PROJECT INFORMATION: In most cases, the joiner pieces will not fit accurately into its space. This is due to inevitable slight variations in glass cutting and assembly angle. Go ahead and cut your glass according to the pattern supplied (it should be slightly larger than the space) and grind it to a perfect fit. (See Joiner Pieces, page 11.)

BROWN'S INLET   by Brian Eagle & Donna Edmondson

DEGREE OF DIFFICULTY

1	2	3	4	**5**

SPECIFICATIONS

# pieces—	164
# sides—	8
Height—	8 1/2" (22 cm)
Bot. Dia.—	20 3/4" (53 cm)
Top Dia..—	3 1/2" (9 cm)

MATERIALS

- — 1 1/2 sq. ft. White Opal
- — 2 1/2 sq. ft. Caramel Opal
- — 1 1/4 sq. ft. Green Opal
- — 1 3/4 sq. ft. Blue Opal

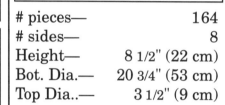

PROJECT INFORMATION: In most cases, the joiner pieces will not fit accurately into its space. This is due to inevitable slight variations in glass cutting and assembly angle. Go ahead and cut your glass according to the pattern supplied (it should be slightly larger than the space) and grind it to a perfect fit. (See Joiner Pieces, page 11.)

DORAN   by Donna Edmondson

DEGREE OF DIFFICULTY

1	2	3	**4**	5

SPECIFICATIONS

# pieces—	162
# sides—	6
Height—	9" (23 cm)
Bot. Dia.—	13 1/2" (34 cm)
Top Dia.—	3" (8 cm)

LAMPBASE

Base height—	12 1/2"
Harp size—	7 1/2"

MATERIALS

- — 3 sq. ft. Mottled White/Green
- — 1 1/2 sq. ft. Mottled White/Clear
- — 1 1/4 sq. ft. White Opal
- — 1/2 sq. ft. Dark Streaky Green
- — 1/4 sq. ft. Green Cath. OR 18 - Sm. Green Nuggets

PROJECT INFORMATION: Each flower skirt panel on this lamp is curved. Use the side of a one gallon paint can (preferably empty) as the form. Attach a copy of the pattern to the can, arrange the foiled glass pieces on the pattern and solder together. Bead solder and clean both the lamp and skirt panels then attach the curved overlay to the assembled lamp skirt at the vertical seams.

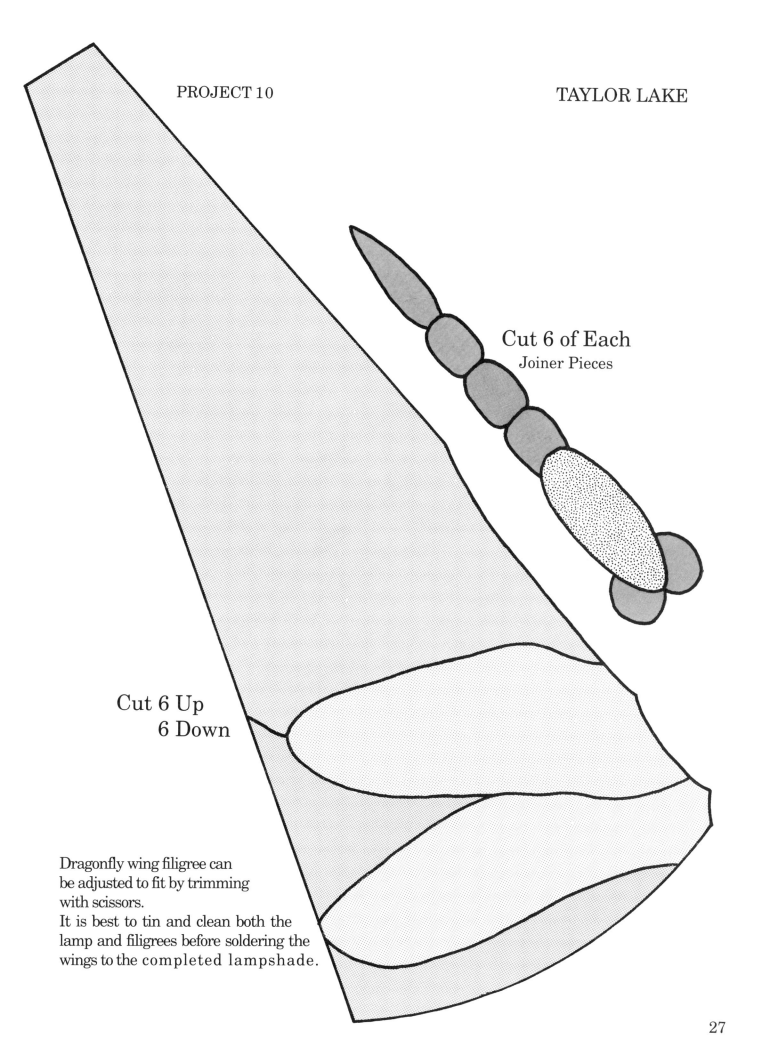

Cut 6 of Each
Joiner Pieces

Cut 6 Up
6 Down

Dragonfly wing filigree can
be adjusted to fit by trimming
with scissors.
It is best to tin and clean both the
lamp and filigrees before soldering the
wings to the completed lampshade.

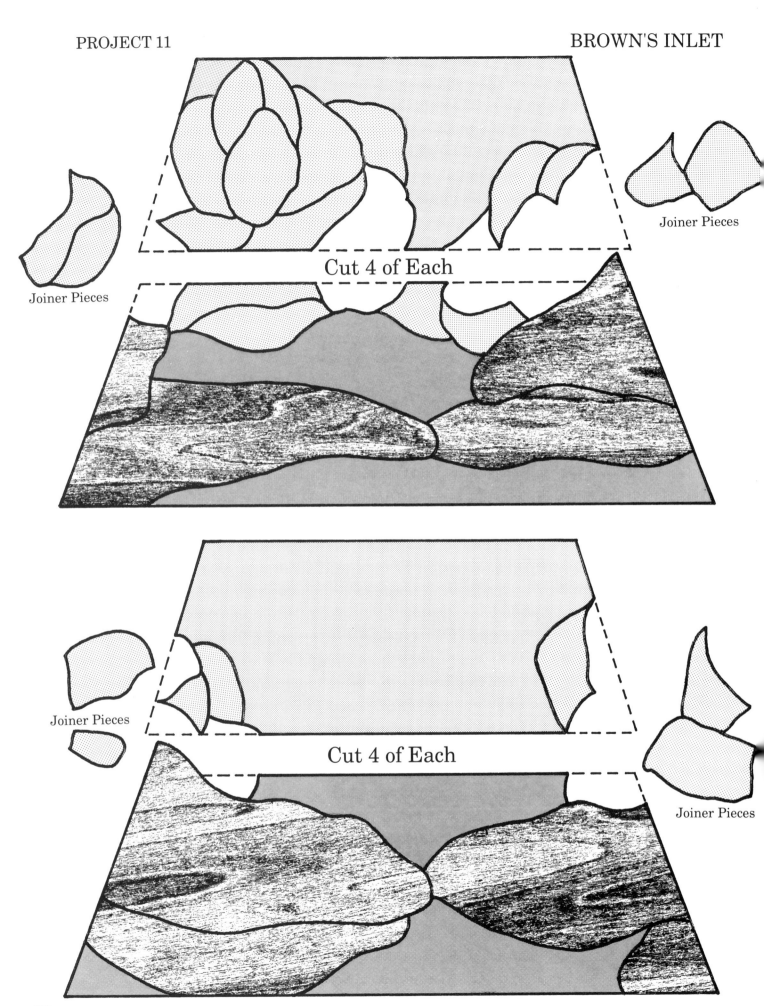

Joiner Pieces

Joiner Pieces

Joiner Pieces

Cut 4 of Each

Joiner Pieces

Joiner Pieces

Cut 4 of Each

Joiner Pieces

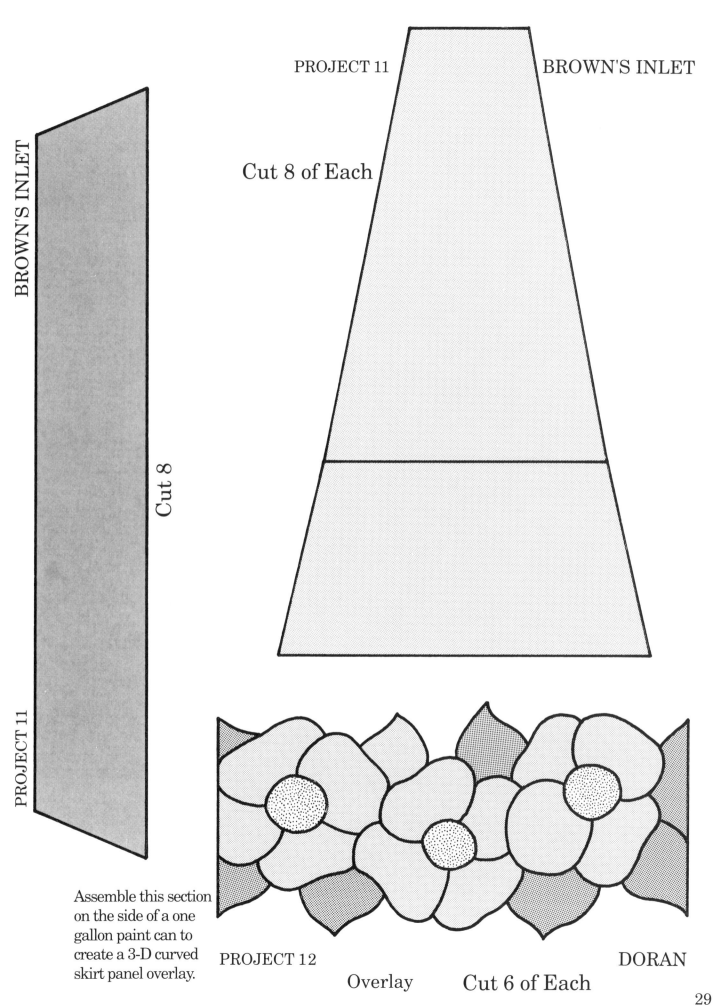

BROWN'S INLET

Cut 8 of Each

PROJECT 11   BROWN'S INLET

Cut 8

PROJECT 11

Assemble this section on the side of a one gallon paint can to create a 3-D curved skirt panel overlay.

PROJECT 12   DORAN

Overlay   Cut 6 of Each

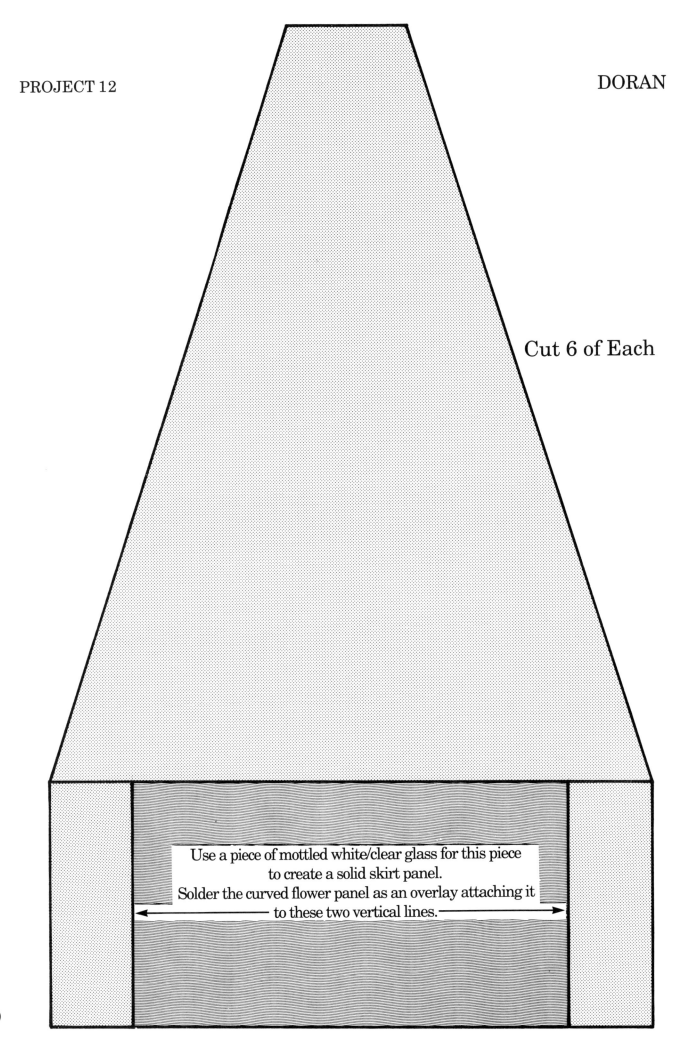

Cut 6 of Each

Use a piece of mottled white/clear glass for this piece
to create a solid skirt panel.
Solder the curved flower panel as an overlay attaching it
to these two vertical lines.

WOLLASTON NORTHERN LIGHTS   by Donna Edmondson

DEGREE OF DIFFICULTY

| 1 | 2 | 3 | 4 | 5 |

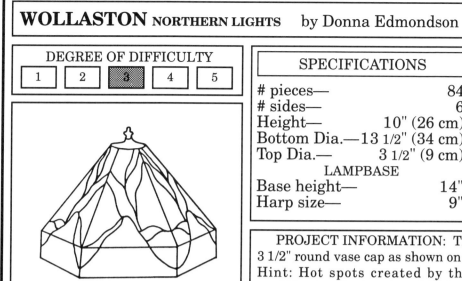

SPECIFICATIONS

# pieces—	84
# sides—	6
Height—	10" (26 cm)
Bottom Dia.—	13 1/2" (34 cm)
Top Dia.—	3 1/2" (9 cm)

LAMPBASE

Base height—	14"
Harp size—	9"

MATERIALS

— 2 1/2 sq. ft. Streaky Black/Clear
— 2 1/4 sq. ft. Dark Blue Cathedral
— 3/4 sq. ft. White Opal
— 3/4 sq. ft. Yellow Cathedral
— 1/2 sq. ft. Orange Cathedral

PROJECT INFORMATION: The top opening can be fitted with a 3 1/2" round vase cap as shown on page 13.
Hint: Hot spots created by the light bulb can be minimized by sandblasting the interior of the lamp after it has been assembled.

ORLEANS   by Gisele Johnson

DEGREE OF DIFFICULTY

| 1 | 2 | 3 | 4 | 5 |

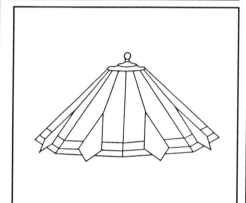

SPECIFICATIONS

# pieces—	56
# sides—	8
Height—	10" (26 cm)
Bottom Dia.—	18" (46 cm)
Top Dia.—	4 1/2" (7 cm)

MATERIALS

— 4 sq. ft. Irid. Streaky White Opal
— 3/4 sq. ft. Pink Cathedral
— Bevels 8 - 6" x 2 3/4" Kites
— 4 1/2 " Vase Cap

PROJECT INFORMATION: Always place the bevels that you have purchased on your pattern and adjust the surrounding pieces where necessary to ensure an accurate fit. After copper foiling we recommend covering both sides of the bevels with masking tape (leaving the foil exposed) to protect them from scratches during assembly.

DORSET   by Barbara Pickthorne

DEGREE OF DIFFICULTY

| 1 | 2 | 3 | 4 | 5 |

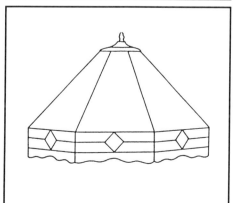

SPECIFICATIONS

# pieces—	56
# sides—	8
Height—	11" (28 cm)
Bottom Dia.—	19 1/2" (50 cm)
Top Dia.—	4 1/2" (11 cm)

MATERIALS

— 6 sq. ft. Pink Craquel Cathedral
— 1 sq. ft. Textured Clear OR Bevels
— 16 - 1" x 4" Left Cnr &
— 16 - 1" x 4" Right Cnr
— 4 1/2" Vase Cap

PROJECT INFORMATION: Always place the bevels that you have purchased on your pattern and adjust the surrounding pieces where necessary to ensure an accurate fit. After copper foiling we recommend covering both sides of the bevels with masking tape (leaving the foil exposed) to protect them from scratches during assembly.

HALIFAX by Ed Kerzner

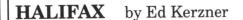

DEGREE OF DIFFICULTY

| 1 | 2 | 3 | 4 | 5 |

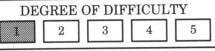

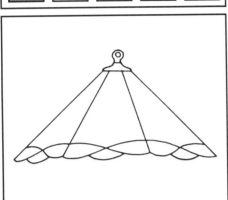

SPECIFICATIONS

# pieces—	32
# sides—	8
Height—	8 1/2" (22 cm)
Bottom Dia.—	17 1/2" (45cm)
Top Dia.—	3 1/2" (9 cm)

MATERIALS

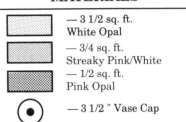

— 3 1/2 sq. ft. White Opal
— 3/4 sq. ft. Streaky Pink/White
— 1/2 sq. ft. Pink Opal
— 3 1/2 " Vase Cap

PROJECT INFORMATION: The top opening can be fitted with either a 3 1/2" eight sided vase cap or a 3 1/2" round vase cap cut to fit as shown on page 13.

FALAISE by Brian Eagle

DEGREE OF DIFFICULTY

| 1 | 2 | 3 | 4 | 5 |

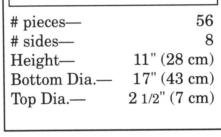

SPECIFICATIONS

# pieces—	56
# sides—	8
Height—	11" (28 cm)
Bottom Dia.—	17" (43 cm)
Top Dia.—	2 1/2" (7 cm)

MATERIALS

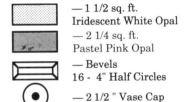

— 1 1/2 sq. ft. Iridescent White Opal
— 2 1/4 sq. ft. Pastel Pink Opal
— Bevels 16 - 4" Half Circles
— 2 1/2 " Vase Cap

PROJECT INFORMATION: Always place the bevels that you have purchased on your pattern and adjust the surrounding pieces where necessary to ensure an accurate fit. After copper foiling we recommend covering both sides of the bevels with masking tape (leaving the foil exposed) to protect them from scratches during assembly.

NORMANDY by Brian Eagle

DEGREE OF DIFFICULTY

| 1 | 2 | 3 | 4 | 5 |

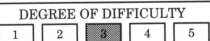

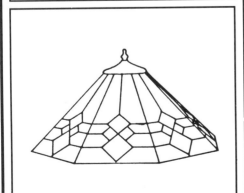

SPECIFICATIONS

# pieces—	96
# sides—	8
Height—	8" (20 cm)
Bottom Dia.—	18" (46 cm)
Top Dia.—	4 1/2" (11 cm)
LAMPBASE	
Base height—	12"
Harp size—	6"

MATERIALS

— 3 1/2 sq. ft. Champagne Opal
— 1 1/2 sq. ft. Teal Textured Cathedral

BEVELS
— 16 - 1" x 1"
— 8 - 1 1/2" x 1 1/2"
— 8 - 2" x 2"
— 4 1/2 " Vase Cap

PROJECT INFORMATION: Always place the bevels that you have purchased on your pattern and adjust the surrounding pieces where necessary to ensure an accurate fit. After copper foiling we recommend covering both sides of the bevels with masking tape (leaving the foil exposed) to protect them from scratches during assembly.

<table>
<tr><td colspan="2">REGENT by Brian Eagle & Donna Edmondson</td><td>PROJECT 19</td></tr>
</table>

DEGREE OF DIFFICULTY

1	2	3	4	**5**

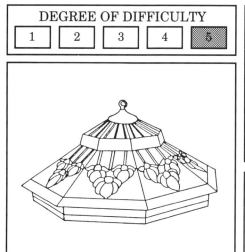

SPECIFICATIONS

# pieces—	312
# sides—	8
Height—	8" (20 cm)
Bottom Dia.—	21" (54 cm)
Top Dia.—	3" (8 cm)

MATERIALS

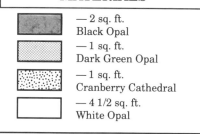

— 2 sq. ft. Black Opal
— 1 sq. ft. Dark Green Opal
— 1 sq. ft. Cranberry Cathedral
— 4 1/2 sq. ft. White Opal

PROJECT INFORMATION: Assemble the main body (flower section including lower trim band) in a jig (see page 7) and begin assembly with these panels. Next add the upper (angled) trim belt (2nd row) then the assembled top row of panels. Attach the vase cap for stability then finish bead soldering the lamp. See page 42 for information on the bottom skirt assembly.

WALL SCONCE MOUNTING & INSTALLATION

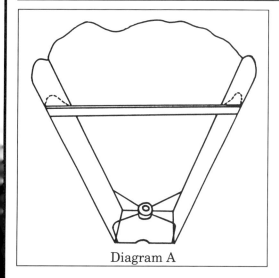

Diagram A

Assemble your wall sconce in the standard flat foil method, as described in the-how to section and finish by installing a mounting / stabilizer bar. The best material for the bar is 1/8" x 3/8" flat zinc coated steel or brass rebar stock (available from your glass supplier). The mounting bar <u>must be</u> soldered to the side panels at the solder joint positioned 2/3 from the bottom (small end) of the sconce. It is very important that this bar be centered & firmly soldered onto these seams, as this bar must hold the weight of the sconce after it is placed on the wall.

There are two methods we recommend to attach your sconce to the wall. One method is to use a wall fixture plate, which is commercially manufactured specifically for stained glass wall sconce installation. This mounting kit, available from many glass suppliers, comes with the wall plate and all necessary electrical parts. Follow the instructions provided with the kit to make sconce installation simple & elegant.

The other method, which we have developed, in the event you have difficulty obtaining a wall fixture plate kit, uses a standard 4 arm lamp spider. Two arms must be bent downward 90° and the other two arms are cut to the appropriate length to fit into the small end of the sconce (see diagram B). Be sure to leave the bent spider arms at least 2" long to allow room for the wiring fixture & socket installation. Tin the end of each spider arm and solder into position as shown in diagram A. Finish by installing a standard candelabra or mini-chandelier socket and cord assembly.

WARNING: When wiring and installing your wall sconce you must consider all federal and local electrical codes and regulations.

To mount your completed sconce on the wall, follow the instructions provided with the wall fixture plate kit. If using the alternate spider method, secure two L hook screws , (see diagram), into the wall, spaced 5"-7" apart (depending on sconce width) on a <u>level</u> horizontal line. Place the sconce on the wall by positioning the mounting bar over the hooks.

Note: If you are mounting the sconce on a gypsum or hard-board dry wall, be sure to use expandable wall board plugs for the screw threads. (Round headed wood screws, left 3/16" out from the wall, can be substituted for the L hooks.)

Diagram B

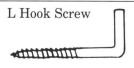

L Hook Screw

Round Head Screw

VICTORIA by Donna Edmondson

DEGREE OF DIFFICULTY

| 1 | 2 | **3** | 4 | 5 |

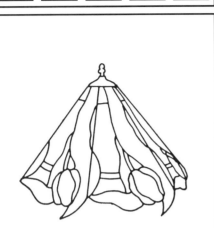

SPECIFICATIONS

# pieces—	84
# sides—	6
Height—	9 1/2" (24 cm)
Bottom Dia.—	15" (38 cm)
Top Dia.—	2 1/2" (6 cm)

LAMPBASE INFORMATION

Base height—	12 1/2"
Harp size—	7 1/2"

MATERIALS

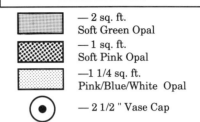

— 2 sq. ft.
Soft Green Opal

— 1 sq. ft.
Soft Pink Opal

—1 1/4 sq. ft.
Pink/Blue/White Opal

— 2 1/2 " Vase Cap

PROJECT INFORMATION: The top opening can be fitted with a 2 1/2" vase cap as shown on page 13. This lamp is suitable for either base or swag.

VICTORIA WALL SCONCE by Donna Edmondson

PROJECT 21

DEGREE OF DIFFICULTY

| 1 | **2** | 3 | 4 | 5 |

SPECIFICATIONS

# pieces—	26
# sides—	3
Depth—	3 3/4" (10 cm)
Height—	10 3/4" (27 cm)
Top Width—	10" (25 cm)

SCONCE INFORMATION

Use a 4 arm spider &
chandelier socket & cord set
or
a wall sconce mount kit.

MATERIALS

— 1/4 sq. ft.
Soft Pink Opal

— 1/2 sq. ft.
Soft Green Opal

— 1 sq. ft.
Pink/Blue/White Opal

REBAR — 12" Long, 3/8" x 1/8"
Flat Rebar

PROJECT INFORMATION: For instructions on Wall Sconce Mounting & Installation see page 33.